M000032962

Wings in Time

Callie Garnett

The Song Cave

The Song Cave
www.the-song-cave.com
© Callie Garnett, 2021
Cover photo by Colm O'Leary

Design and layout by Janet Evans-Scanlon

All rights reserved. Printed in the United States of America.
No part of this book may be used or reproduced in any manner whatsoever
without written permission except in the case of brief quotations embodied
in critical articles and reviews. Members of educational institutions and
organizations wishing to photocopy any of the work for classroom use, or
authors and publishers who would like to obtain permission for any material
in the work, should contact the publisher.

ISBN: 978-1-7372775-0-7
Library of Congress Control Number: 2021941572

FIRST EDITION

Contents

[Serial Mom]   1

i. Wings in Time   7

ii. The Yellow Notebook   41

iii. Scraps of Chalk   51

iv. My Stalker Luke Gotschalk   75

Notes   93

Acknowledgments   97

Serial Mom

If obsession arrests you in time
Consider me ten, when I turned to mom & said
Can we just look in the video store?

It was a schoolnight.

Movies are a Hot medium, says Marshal McLuhan:
Hi data, hi def
Highly involving, asking little of you.

(To McLuhan the telephone was Cool
Imagine)

The video store between 7th & 8th was easy to case
Quickly and linger in
John Candy on the North Wall, to the East

A room set off by a curtain of wooden beads.
I remember thinking, *who are you kidding?*
I've seen behind the beads (I never had).

★

The cover of *Last Tango in Paris*:
Flesh-colored
& steamy, somehow like video itself.

The cover of *The Money Pit*:
A mussed up couple standing by a big nice house.
The house was a money pit.

The cover of *The Fisher King* was such a mystery to me:
Just a man laughing
By a pond
With a ponytail.

The cover of Steve Martin's *The Jerk* was almost too good to be true:
The jerk himself

& the night we chose to bring him home
I got a little scared.

The cover of *Bedknobs and Broomsticks* showed
Children riding a bed through the sky w/ Angela Lansbury
Who's not even hiding the fact that she's a witch.
> Why hide? There's a war on & you have these
> Special skills.

The cover of *I Married a Witch* showed a concerned-looking man.
I Married a Communist, same. *Serial Mom*:
> A mom
> Grinning widely
You had to be careful who you married.

★

Mom actually worked at *Sesame Street*.
There *were* googly eyes scattered everywhere
Matted hair of red & blue, reedy puppeteers . . .

Mom, why is the man on the TV pulling apart the calzone?
> I don't know.
There's a lot on TV that doesn't involve you.

For McLuhan, TV is a Cool medium.
It seems right that we, now, should pass the time coolly
In a hot context.

The cover of *The Good Son* with Macaulay Culkin
You just knew he wasn't good.

★

Dear Mom,

It so upset you when unwholesome rumors spread about
Mister Rogers' Neighborhood.

> *Fred was a saint*, you said. & we wept

When he addressed the Senate Subcommittee on Communication.
Children's Television as a kind of religion. Often

You could have a Muppet's carriage, easing through the house
Like Prairie Dawn or a rock snail reaching

Sun.
　　　The rare Saturday you slept in
I might take out your broom, my broom

While I watched cartoons.
Cartoons are Cool media, as you will have gathered by now, for I
swept the living room
Through them.

i. Wings in Time

Wings in Time

I

In Eric's latest missive is a tercet that chills me to the roots of my hair.
Every mother is famous / And hated if they don't beat their / Wings in time
with the infant.

I wonder if he's right when he writes: *Fame mothers*—surely mothers
arm, enflame.
I hear Henry's new kitten Sabine is fearful & moist from toilet
condensation.
My mother is ruminative. Only in my dreams do I become unchewed.

And there,
How gross,
I long for what I know—all my desires felt overused and sterile like a
diesel pump, like
a man soaked in cheap brandy. The desire to be looked at naked, taken in,
warmed.
I slept too much, fitfully, more dreams of

Chicago, that broad & empty city of many
invisible bros getting invisible blowjobs.

In one dream I just replay a familiar scene from the Blue Line, where a boy we thought was blowing himself gets knocked back by the jostling, & is blue.

At the station, after the medics come, *into that mood of hypocrisy & cynicism, pouring scorn all over,* my fellow riders and I fall.

I am happy for my poems my blood to have a local circulation—
I like talking to you,
I like talking to you too.

                    (little juke box with an Out of Order sign)

This wanton scatter of lines isn't poetry.

If I die and live again I'll say it again:

I am a media child. I speak in the language of movies and TV.

II

In one video, Kermit and Elmo act out Happy and Sad. They keep
switching places like pugilists. Kermit's bearing stays the same while
Elmo's swings wildly, manically.
Somebody could lose a hand.

In the added slo-mo and grainy close-up the truth settles on Elmo.

How somberly, how curtly my little niece says *MORE* when we sing *E
I E I O* for the last time
As if punishing the food pellet button.

*I washed with the chemicals they gave me to wash with / I felt the feelings I was
given to feel*

I know you think I'm addicted to the chemicals, the feelings, but truly
I am not
I am not.

The conifers behind the house move for the wind, look.
I only care because you would, because you go mad, you must go mad
for that sort of thing.

How will I spot a bird without you? How will I know what's pregnant
in nature? How will I be ever pregnant myself?

By sitting inside, reading Hopkins?
googling Matchbox Twenty to prove my little niece looks like Rob
Thomas?
scowling, like, *It's 3am I must be lonely*? How will I know if a poem is
any good without you?

No one else will tell me, or they'll tell me too straight.

You are my out of doors.

My name is Sweetheart, I said, waking on the gurney. *I know
my first name is Sweetheart.*

III

Eric and I thought we'd try a correspondence
the kind that poets do to help each other write
But Eric, it's just this:

The conifers behind the house move for the wind.

I have nothing to look at in my quarantine. Anemic. I can't even stand
out there.

I stumbled on a word yesterday, *panegyric*, and I really had to rack my
brain.
My brain said: *I don't know.*

I didn't look it up because what's the point? Everywhere you go there's
more words.

Perhaps panegyric is a horn, gyre-like litany of praise such as desperate
poetry slobbers.
Great Panegyrics!
To the unsuspecting dead and lost.

Perhaps it can turn the other way too.
Making you cry in the shower, thinking: *Where shall I go?*

Why am I not a gondolier?
or a fisherman with a little lateen?

The earth is large but I already know
I'll exhaust every road, I'll empty every scene

In the end
Melody will know me better than I know myself.

IV

A picture of me from before I knew you: I'm sitting at a computer at the record store—a bit of North Linn St. behind me.

The owner, Craig, wears black, a long-white ponytail, goatee, violet-tinted glasses, and a beanie. For every CD in the store he has me print a representative.

I scan the cover and back cover into a doc and size them. This I print, cut, and slip into a stiff laminate. And *that* goes in the browsing crates by genre. Such analog shopness!

It's backwards, I thought. *I like this. And after all I didn't invent it, it fits into the customs.*

Craig had two or three shopgirls.
To one of the younger ones I remember saying: "It's not *'in media ray'* it's *'en medias res*,' you say it with the S"

As I said it I knew I was wrong
and in her frustration, her acne, her angry eyes I saw us both losing grandly, comically to education.

It's funny how ground down I look. I pity

myself for not knowing you yet
except as passing through, how I hate
the idea of you now
like the merch that came with new releases every week—a little poster
of some dipshit Mumford & his sons.

V

Craig taught his girls in sound, maybe. I'd sometimes pick him up on
the air, mid one of his calm, completist rolls on bop.
Truly he had a voice for radio.

And I could almost work up longing for him, such is the power of the
soft box
mastery that does not visibly read from cards

but steals touches of my knee and shoulder, hair, through which I too
was on the radio, in the knowledge.

But it was dinky work: you'll recall I'd print the image I'd just
scanned, from the disc I'd just held in my hand, to find the Deutsche
Gramophones was tricky

It's funny how struck down I look. I learned about Art Pepper
Michael
Hurley . . .

These are broken men, listen for yourself.

"For now, Craig gets to have his storefront, girls, pipe, and cinnamon
bun, but soon
he'll go online, all this will go online," said his wife one day, laying it
out for me.

And so it did

her sharp hippie earring swung like it could (grudge) never evaporate

I remember looking down at her sandaled feet while I felt our cameos
collide, and she felt it,
her costume in mine, and my mind went blank.

Mother? I thought.
Teacher?
Girlfriend?
Lawyer?
Crone?

Married to a petty nobleman & third rate musician

I pulled out Ethel Waters on vinyl (for the records were there; they
stood for themselves).

Occasional Poem

This was the occasion: A Zebra
Of a virus showed up on horsefeet,
Showed up differently in each body
The way we all have different shoes.
1 person infected 2, 2 4, 4 8, and so on;
We had to stay indoors.

I camped with my family,
                              invisible bomb.

At that time, perhaps more than any other,
I wished to hear myself singing.
But a sense of shakiness pervaded
I felt I must appear to clutch at voice.

I watched old films instead, thought about you
Suffered from what many at the time called the Folly
Or the Need,
Or the Folly of the Need,
Where *everything* reminds me I won't grow
All the *Little Women* films: 1933, 1949, 1994, 2019.
Everything reminds me of you but you
Don't know.
Men never know what
                              little women means.

Katherine Hepburn's Jo is nimble and stiff
June Allyson's, a poor man's, loud
Until she steps out of her
                    home
As if all speech before was spam / the tin peels from her rations can

Only who knows what longing is
Will know me.

                    The virus possibility
                    is heavy today; I sense a reclamation
Of the past occurring, so remotely,

but what past?

                    June's Chestnut hair, her sexual
                    orientation is bearded artist. I get it, I'm the same.

I read about a woman whose life in ninety
Seconds changed.
Well,   mine is changing
                         slowly.

A matins squawk sets off almost no reaction.
My little niece, not learning to speak, wags
Her head, wearing invisible mask.
She loves the part that you're not supposed to play with:
Remainders and labels

She loves tags,   like the tags on Alph and Ralph,
                        her dogs.

Grass is sort of tags. She
                        will probably love grass.

Quarantine Fascinations

Lilacs, song, *Outbreak*, *Heat*
Yeats, Piano, *Mildred Pierce*
The Bridges of Madison County, *Sesame Street*, *November*, Birdsong
Simone de Beauvoir, Kate Millet, feminist, Chris Nealon, poet,
Diderot, frenchman
Waxahatchee, creek, Brandon Brown. poet, Flaubert, frenchman
Marie Howe, *Copycat*, The Seven Devils, poem, earth, world, globe, planet

Terms of Endearment

Shake Your Sillies Out
That's how little babies think, reprimand
wharf, dock, A child loves me, fact

Coffee, Pecans, Cigarettes & Coffee, song, dock, quay, pier, Muscle Shoals
Clarence Carter, Patches, song, I Must Become a Menace to My
Enemies, poem
Diderot, opulent cynic, globe, planet, wharf, dock, quay, pier, *Mildred
Pierce*, novel,
Outbreak, pandemic, Yeats, Irishman, Cake, Inventory, ritual, *The
Butcher's Wife*

The Preacher's Wife, *Throw Mama from the Train*, *Big Business*, *Serial Mom*,
The Fugitive, video
Frankie & Johnny, Lilacs, patchouli, Piano, hobby

The Bridges of Madison County, loneliness
Marie Howe, Sesame Street, corporate paper, Glimpsing, eyeing

Not having to search for a word like earth, innocence, world, globe,
Coffee, drug
Pecans, That's how little babies think, Obama wisdom, Happy
Graduation Days, One by One

Lilacs, song, *Heat*
Yeats, Piano, *Sesame Street, November*, Birdsong

Humor in Fiction

they had this character, fatty arbuckle,
licking pumpkin pie off of this woman's vagina
his tongue going the wrong way
that's not how you eat pussy
I felt it in my stomach

was a time, I think they were trying to say, *appetite was appetite*
Hollywood gossip: I spend the summer in a coffee-breath scented N95
dust mask
with my folks

★

in light of the new public social, here's how
I'll talk to you, let's talk about how soap
operas have the whole world mesmerized
even me

free-spirited Debra Winger in 1983,
Terms of Endearment,
looking worried, flushed, a purple sweatband
why did I make this brutal move from Houston to Des Moines?

it's hard without you
I drag road metal
become disorganized
forget how the bridge goes

★

Debra, lead me back along the stream out of town
behind the lot behind Shaw's
the grocery box

at the farthest reaches of the community often occur new Shaw's
as though Nature plays with greater freedom secretly
at the edges of the world

sometimes I wish I'd met you on a big ship
hidden speakers everywhere, behind the fronds
you told me to go out and get some confidence
I feel like a real sportsman wouldn't do that

★

after the panel in San Antonio, Humor in Fiction,
it was mythical: Jake's tall frame belittled the Alamo

he kicked over a water machine
filled with off-brand water

This can't be the actual Alamo but it was

such military sites, old and public...
it's like we're fighting for a bad view

I started to be able to really feel my engine rev
understood the impulse as an intricate system

and then right outside Forever 21 w/ the
weathered saloon doors, Jake said

why don't you just buy a bathing suit?
everything works out,

I'll remember this day forever

Responses like autobiography, we concluded,
must themselves be undergoing dramatic changes.

    ★

but to spend anything
resembling leisure time at a panel is a joke for the gods
Humor in Fiction

I sat next to a prison guard in plain clothes
I knew him like a fox knows goose holes

you weren't there, so I'll tell it forever
the story of the panel, Humor in Fiction
in such rooms, *my soul runs to seed, boredom takes over,*
all they know of happiness is the part which cloys first

Macedonia Road

for Jess

I like music because I like sound
that makes me feel, said the Peloton instructor,
a former make-up artist, attentive to detail,
who knows not of me but pushed me hard
and never let me fall.

After,
as I crossed the grass, demented
from keeping time with my butt
I wondered, is it ok to just say to Jess
how much I love her energy?

What you drink / gets into your mouth / becomes saliva
You're alive
and all living drama takes place within a few vertical miles, totally
scannable by the naked eye
except for tree frogs, which one rarely sees.

I took a long walk out country roads: down Reed where I've walked
with Jess before,
turned onto Beale where the woods are thicker, had a little scare when
a truck rolled by, unhurried.

It's a little confusing, isn't it, Jess (we can now acknowledge)?
To be a woman in her mid-thirties with a pretty cute ass
walking on the road alone at sundown
out of earshot—panic,
shame at the panic.

Some driveways have
a security system decal
screwed to a tree, one called CIA (the display is by subscription—
you can just pay for the sign).

So happy birthday.

Anyway I turned around, walked back, turned onto Macedonia Road.

Suddenly bits of chat flew out of the quiet (first cocktails after months
of isolation).
Don't go, said everyone ever.

It was like arriving at a party.

I made out a small man in hot pink shirt and shorts yelling
Shut up
with real ire at a pair of geese.

Birds were singing on every tree.
Tanagers, mostly, lined up on the boughs as the sunset

yellowed them the MORE.
All nature seemed inclined for
the dimming wall before a rest, and

I thought of the 1972 bestseller,
The Secret Life of Plants, a work of dubious science beloved by poets,
where the flowers and tomatoes took lie detector tests,
admitted they were really sylphs
hoping to move out West.

AirBnB

A tree with zit-sized holes drilled up its trunk
Drunk on neglect
Is flowering.

Mendocino clouds cling and loosen
Smoky cock, parting from balls.

Don't worry,
That squeak in the wind is just boughs adjusting.

I adjust to a house by taking the trash out barefoot
Bringing its nervous system down
To low hum.

Here's the remote on a slip of paper.
Rules and codes.

The Great San Bernardino Pitch Party

Noah Purifoy Outdoor Art Museum

I'm interested in feminist oratory, we think
Jess should say
Specifically that.

Yellow-breasted engine sounds on the
Joshua tree
Joshua tree mid-shimmy

I think every bird is mad
At me. Does that make me
An alcoholic?

What is the pitch, you might ask
A heart of dryness?
It's gritty, it's raw, it's new, it's an underside view

It's a book about a man who changed the landscape
(Draft pitch for Duchamp)

Your rhetorical smile 3 hours outside LA
Under the desert sky
After

The great San Bernardino sculpture party

Sparkling toilet pieces lay tiled into
The pavilion,
Silver flushers too.

Comic mounds of bowling balls
Sociable rows of washer dryers

TV piles. I am
Uneasy. So what?
No match for the always sand and always

Air. I find a pair of leather pants
Hanging in a hut & touch them.
Definitely not leather.

Pitch
It's also a substance

I can see the sunscreen on your face
Not rubbed in,
Tears wetting

Your under-chin. *Let's get this next pitch*
Right, guys.

Love Street, L.A.

I've been learning piano in quarantine, so this
is not really related, but
I have to say it:

Jim Morrison was a hack.

Why bury him next to Balzac?
His rhymes were bad, his eyes unintelligent.
　　try to run, try to hide / break on through to the other side

designed as a woman's retreat.

Is it especially lame for a woman
to write about fame *now*? Confusion about

who lived on Love Street. (*She* did.)
who lives on Love Street? (*She* does.)
E flat to C minor . . . I don't know.

I pass even my darlings when I'm
on a roll down the avenue. F minor to D
to C; C to D to B flat

♪ *Lookout Mountain Avenue / you're a movie I can put my hand into* ♪
That would be one of my songs.
Lookout Jim Morrison, you road toad, dick flinger, wannabe drone.

Like Geffen I'll go to work when this is done,
consider 300 emails.
On any given day I might say both of these:

so compelling / I don't have a vision for how to break it out in the market
A song about cruising really is about my life;
all of these poems are, even if

they seem quite scrappy,
filled with references,
anachronisms.

Dear Eric

Can they hear me through the wall?, because
what I'm playing / singing softly / haltingly
is magnificent
B to C sharp minor to E
& it's miserly; I'll never do it in public

I keep thinking of that time you visited me in the retired
living room
their plants looked neglected & green
I realized from your eye on mine:
Anything we make could happen between us now
mosquito netting

> *What stars there were shrunk, even as they multiplied*
> It
> *Seemed a very bad, anxious ode to redistribution*

I caught two, maybe three, shooting
I follow me in my wake and you complete the system
like an uncle, indifferent

> *I won't die if I don't change, just live a dead life*

Dear Eric,

Your last poem, with the phrase *glue in the swipes*
Makes me want to wipe my fingers.

As a lonely person, I appreciate being called *independent*
My little niece *gasping* with love for me

gray crayon
rolled from one end of the paper to the other.

She makes bird caws. Her caws could respond or command.
I think they command.

We must never confuse the truth with what happens
don't you think so, remakes?

Remakes, you are a flea disturbing my peace.
You are a terrible terrible terrible

mosquito.

Keeping Time

I think you might appreciate tomatoes
emit a squeal heard by the tomato family.

All some butterflies know is songs, & poems, & they hear
bits of wisdom, snatches of verse and melody.

My brother-in-law is a drummer, *Grief is clarity*, he said to me last night,
and people without children are themselves children.

I realize keeping time is serious.
Have you ever tried it?

As this story demonstrates,
a child is life gasping out
of the bog

but there's something about the bog alone I like.

You have to practice constantly.
It's always trying to throw you off.

I get to know my cuticles well, and nail beds
other sites of excrescence.

I see Katherine Hepburn in the Peloton screen,
    you didn't have Peloton, I say
We did, she says,

    but not with the screen and stuff

and she tells me this story: that for 3 whole days the girl lies piteously
    on the narrow lounger in her parents' yard,
    as if the sun could melt her involvement.

    on the 4th day her mother says, *let's go get a
    manicure*, & she goes to appease her
    mother, even though she likes not painting
    her own

    she tilts her head back
    away from the foot chairs
    then maybe these tears will leave
    I'm gonna keep listening until I'm petrified

Why can't I be intimate?

I feel so unindpired.

scandal is aboslutely necessary to melodrama.

what's a grass widow?

someone who has to pay for all her pleasures with rouble.

memorable troubl.

as we got out past kensington we got loose about which firends of the other we'd sleep with.

I managed to like you were sleeping with on eor two others

it gave you a dress, a suit.

Because a magzine says it saps pimples, a naif puts peach yogurt on her face.

Did she go to the pier to end her life?

or just to be near the restaurants and trucked in laundry?

Show me your most American traits.

it's one of my main adtaptatio tricks.

that contraption waitresses clip their orders on and spin ino the kitchen

ii. The Yellow Notebook

There she goes again
In her athletic shoes & visor
Up the hill backwards

Every day she goes
Every sunny day
Up the hill backwards

Sometimes I worry it will stunt
The child
(Not a research-based
concern, just a feeling)

The notebook started practically
But then

I kept wanting to have it
It looked good today, all-day

Goldenrod yellow it was, as
The packaging on skid grease

Of pocket dimensions, like a
Clock:

I started wherever and crashed into the morning

It was a lot like a process:

I kept losing the notebook,
Leaving it around my section,

On the steel berm,
By the mud pot

(In a funny way I kept discarding it)

When a *blonde in sand* needed both my hands,

Meatloaf specials, *hold the*
Paint & pin roses on

I set my finger short
That's my time, I've hit my number

The yellow notebook had slightly rounded
corners

Sometimes I'd set my finger there
As if to let a bug crawl off

Streak it
2 rafts w/ sunny, 3
Rolling pebbles, the regs

Vile Campers
Hold the ice

Nice
Hairclip

(My niece baked it)

Make it ugly

Knife, creamer, napkin box
Extra Bronx vanilla

She's as bad as I remember

She stacks

She marries the low ketchups

Like they're lonely

I wanted to buy the bird shift
The blue shift, the shift where I bare my arms

I wanted to buy a star too
The big one

At that time I kept many tattered notebooks
Above the cheekbones and below the chin

When I had a thought worth recording I simply grabbed one.
I kept no track of them nor in them of what they contained.
So that once in a yellow notebook can only be sloppy
I considered this deliberate
Fermentation. Seasonal even. What smells good
will be rooted out. I am the pig in this scenario
& so are others.

I thought often of a video of a woman preparing kimchi in her small
practical kitchen. But I also thought of other women I had seen, living
in disarray.

Not really like a process. It was always in a different bag or drawer. So
many bags books come in. Cloth-bound.

Seriously scrappy poems.

Concordance

Yellow is the color of relinquishment

Yellow as a rule appears in sickness

Shone yellow through the square and narrow streets

Bobbing up like blazons in fog

Example of a phrase that does not deepen:
"An ush of sound"
What is this "ush"?

It does not deepen

iii. Scraps of Chalk

> *"If we accept the premise that commercials are effective teachers*
> *it is important to be aware of their characteristics."*
> —Joan Ganz Cooney, Co-Creator of "Sesame Street"

A friendly-looking pirate rolls out a baby carriage full of gear

Another pirate lugs a bulky Panasonic through the grass

Maybe a Sony Portapak. I don't know. Most things aren't worth
describing

Invasive how they let the kid wear his own turtle shirt,

Leave his hesitations in? (his mistakes)

At certain colors and textures of their invention his gaze occasionally
gleams

He does not thrive with every question

He utters a passionate set of ums

Like a truck backing up

I get sore jealous of the network, of the spot, and the next one

Though they give their love so evenly

The Grid of Intimacy

Behold: A vegetarian with his hand up a

Heavy equipment, which is The Count

His deathless numbers! How I loved them

And the night we were allowed to take him home

From the Sesame Workshop

I got a little scared.

He weighed more than you'd think.

When Linda Rondstadt

Asks Elmo for a hug, Elmo considers.

Dear Mom,

The year of your birth

Marked the first significant break in movie

Self-censorship in more than 20 years.

Hugh Hefner founded *Playboy*,

An entertainment monthly for indoor urban males 18-80

51 copies of the first issue,

Containing nude photographs

Of Marilyn Monroe,

Sold for 50 cents each.

Touching Elmo's fur brings out the dog in Elmo

As surely as throwing a bone

Confusing, consenting, ticklish.

Inspiration

"Inspiration is there all the time . . .
    It is a consolation even to plants and animals"
    —Agnes Martin

What did I do to get this needs?
Today I got a squeaky nut

I go to the Met
Cute how I go

Where I know bones & skulls will be
Zurbaran's lemons in her hamper

The first time I recognized
A lemon of Zurburan I thought

Now I have been transformed by art
I mean it

He wasn't the most prolific
Or best Spaniard but

There is a genius in transition

I spent maybe 40 minutes there
And saw no other poet

*

Did you leave a bunch of stuff at my house?
The child said

Hair in my brush?
Anyway now it's my stuff

What is this?
The child sassed

This doesn't seem like ordinary grass

*

I had a string of girls I might called friends
Elena, Elena, (two named Elena)

All tough, brunette, lizardy
Quick of movement

They considered me tentative
As the harvesters

As the harvesters
Follow arrows of crop

Be open to them, they told me of boys
Of parting

All had brothers
Even their sisters were brothers

Their mothers were brothers with snacks

Their fathers were a distant
Sort of brothers

I was very up front
I said, Elena, *Praise makes me very happy*

Glory holds no emptiness for me

One had threadbare underwear and loved to dip
Into olive oil anything

★

Did I invent poetry?
Asked the child

What if I just write things dad says?

How much sense do I have to make?

One time dad said moonlight is pale
Speaking of something else

Are poems neurotic twitches?
Sassed the child
Is everything art?

For example,
We ate pork belly and the tree
Doubled over like a knee

A sudden big smell in nature
Turns out to be Big Red,
White pepper and mulch

I hope not

& the flags of dusk rise up
& the sky expands past its pokey threads

Then I remember the word for this place.

Imagination

A wealthy couple from NYC is passing through
West Virginia
When suddenly their twins need to be born.

The local factory hospital is only for factory
Employees
So the rich man buys the factory, & his wife delivers

There. Exactly then, so does a factory wife. Twins.
What astonishing timing! Both sets must be fraternal.
They don't match. Later,

One woman's love of rocking chairs deforms her
In midtown,
In the board room, in the OTIS elevator down.

Likewise, what's amiss with a country girl in gingham who
Turns away
Men covered in pig shit (nicely, she's not snooty)

And is giddy to stroll the Avenue? To be in the wrong
Place is to collect
Rays of light long passed, a compact disc in the night

Trash. To be in the right place is to grow
So that
Wherever you are appears to be the center.

I'll tell you: This Easter morning I find Grand
Hotel
Lobbies alive with sisters like pinballs, like Lucilles.

One sister might be an outfit, a clerk
Or hiss with a herder's ardor
Or lead workers;
One might depart The Carlisle
On business,
Uncoupled.

Insolence

Who is this mythic creature
Who lives so poetry?
Oh, it's Abby the pink muppet.

Book where she goes to the store.
I don't much go for it. I didn't
Have the courage to talk

About urban history then. My teacher
Would cover her cup
Because we spit? The headmaster spit

When he ate while
Speaking a vending
Machine pastry as though

(Intently)
To a small piece of dough.
Other flecks on the scene:

"jungle gym"
dome
"May pole": Ribbons on a metal pole

"Why did you stop feeding my turtle?"
He seemed to be saying
Or something like that.

What does it mean, *Everywhere*
She goes she leaves
A trail of magic?

Is her Viking ship in lightning?
Everywhere *I* go I leave a trail
But that's different.

Is it
Because you want to go so bad?
If you don't want to go is it still

A trail of magic?
If you *really* want to is it not?
My teacher tells me spiritual

Abuse is abuse
Of the spirit.
Is it inside? I think it's

You get your clothes
All dusty for nothing.
Returning from the war you'll catch

Bits of popcorn in the aisles
The whole arrangement garish
In the flashlight, Hunger

At the scene of the feast.
We read a book about a gymnast
Girl whose fall gives her a blood

Transfusion gives her disease
It had a white cover.

And you find in self-denial you have nurtured
Only blame

Like a deep deep *complaint*
Upon the lilies.
Says Montaigne:

"Saying is a different thing
From doing; the preaching &
The preacher aren't the same"

But I don't see how they aren't
The same. What a tedious and hackneyed
Translation is this

Past
Which angers me & disfigures my face.
It's not that my friends won't know me

They will.

Hospitality

It's important to me that I age

into a woman of power.
The dowager strokes the terrier, & is not barred from snooping

into any of the Wings
of human experience.

On the Potential Uses of
Television for the Preschool Mind

1. Ability to name
Positive and negative
Instances of tools or
Furniture or farm equipment.

Tell me something that is
Not a weapon.
A cow is not a weapon.

Tell me a gun.

2. Ability to apply these concepts
locally.

Is a crayon a piece
Of a weapon or furniture?
No a crayon is not.

3. There should be evidence
That the printed word has
Some meaning for the child

The same as what is pictured

As number has amount.

4. Ability to count aloud
To 20 without help, and to 100
With just a hint at the decade
Points (30, 40)

5. And at least 15 consonants.

leeeeks, hrrrrd, offffp Q

6. There should be evidence of
Reasoning.
Is this a thing that goes
Mrow?

7. Ability to produce a
Word that
Rhymes with a blank:

I had a dog and his
Name was Abel. I found

Him hiding under the

_____.

8. Ability to describe
Arrangements: on the,
Between the,

9. Art teachers
Have found that children
Rather well depict
Abstractions at this point.

One child was able to draw
How it feels when it rains on me

—and talent
Gathers about them.

10. Pretendo,
A skilled and ageless mime,
Showed
Them how to

Curl up like seeds
Tight on the ground
In the winter,

Slowly unfold
Like little lentil sprouts
In spring

How to grow and blossom
In the summer,

Wilt in fall, return
To the ground.

(One child was able to say
How it feels when it rains on me:
It rains past me.)

I forget what I'm watching
That I'm watching.

12. This is not the time
To torment them with
Mechanics.

But the concept
Say, a rudimentary account
Of how to get a rocket
Into outer space

They should be able to
Manage.

Remember that Advantage has been gained
From their entertainments; having
No clue where apples
Come from

Grover is able to build
a machine with
a mouse,
a little wheel,
cooperation,
a dusty fan,
a slide, a trough,
a boat, and cheese.

This is known as

Scrapcraft,
Giving life to household
Objects, which serves another
Crucial aptitude,

Getting rid of trash

You have to want
to

Share with people.

13. Ability to touch
The screen and *CHAIR*
Lights up

And after a few
Seconds, the host
Says, *that's right*.

iv. My Stalker, Luke Gotschalk

I undid the Velcro at his cuff,
Yelled out a number and smelled his legs while Chicago breathed him

Shoe funk, ankle scar
The retractable shelf
Navel

I inserted with my hands
A tampon
Don't get him in me, I thought

Luke Gotschalk

I.

He's really
He's
He must be peering into my life at this point, my stalker

His name is Luke Gotschalk and he's writing everywhere
he's causing writing everywhere
like a moth beats its wings against a screen

*it's like there's a scrap of glory in me I was asked to keep safe while the world
goes to hell.*

I keep prying the walls of safety up
and away
                    to get a look at things

Click through to his sources, you'll find
a wall of pictures, young white *beautiful girl*-women

I find them on the wall
behind things
in basements at police stations

her skin is like a brown peach with the yellow *on*

Purple, red, and green handprints behind her on the wall
she rests her folded arms
on a bright red drop cloth, for making
on a fine fabric, for owning

I keep thinking of history, blowing the new women
around in a test room

II.

how did you find me, Luke Gotschalk?

the last thing I saw lassoed was a woman,
female

I go looking for the clip online
become all fizzy with media, each new work of art
speaking my name

> is a mother what i was meant to be
> i already have a mother child
> who slaughters me with kindness/niceness

the special way niceness becomes sickness, loves power
loves sickness
> (I would never, by the way, eliminate niceness for being bland.)

I swear because it tastes sweet in my mouth
like yellow wine
did you find me from the picture where I'm a witch?

could you send that by media mail, that feeling?
children and other communications
so easy to replace

in which reactions happen

media, I hear the ends are always kissing

my heart filling up, spilling over
i'm getting heart on my chin
media I'm in the middle, watching]]]

III.

There are 51 Lucas Gotschalks on Facebook
doesn't that seem like a lot?

83 if you count the slight spinoffs
Luke Gotschall
who's making all these?

A theory of children:
they predict me

I'd already been the very small parent of a very big child—my mother, said
Gloria Steinem

she looks ready to get serious
education is a set of possibilities
but am i an education to my child?

The story of a girl: I gazed on her, her haircut, chalkboard, projector
screen rolled down over it, professor, a large deep purple quote from
Marguerite

Duras was becoming dots
politely, media is happening

A story from my education: i learned what a blog was in a house with
wallpaper
one of the weird rooms for weird girls

could a wall be generated
in hyperspace, one girl asked

in seminar one morning, to deliver poetry in moving fonts, colors & sizes
and at different speeds? what about with branches?

(no one spoke yet of Hovering)   (these are possibilities)

a wall could be generated, I continued, in hyperspace, to generate
poetry itself
a block of it, forever

IV. Ari, You Can Stand

Ari, you can stand here in Berlin in my doorway, watch how money
comes, in
realness real reality, you sit already in the plane, it's sent back
programme in sense of money, on
17th July 2020 business / woman in my art is over AT all.

Now the 17th of July is exactly two weeks away. A Friday.
firework time and with the anticipation
I started really being able to feel my engine rev

it wasn't a person who turned me on
now that i've made my decision, I do not want your
little glass

jar with dregs of gold paint in it
a feeling of riding history
opportunistically
on the rolling edge
and the pens
my hand in fate's hand
We'll be lovers in the open.

I'll support you
fight for you
yeah, just pick a thing
that'll be *your thing*

V. They Tell Me I'm a Muppet

How do I not be a muppet?

First of all how do I not be a puppet?

MOM: There is a cardinal in our dogwood tree. It is a great combination.

Nearer to the end of Nestra,

Full moon, bitter gland

> *I loved how the women danced*

Full moon, bitter gland

VI. Independence Day

Tiffany showed me the spacious outdoor porch and porch furniture,
and the spacious house, excitedly,
a house (20 miles away, in Hillsdale) I was proud to arrive at, so limited
is my driving

she showed me including the owner's rotund chihuahua, Sean, golden brown
and offered me a diet coke,

ending in a green hub, the village, where i recognize that dim ice
cream shop (many things are closed)
where blue light hit that scooper

round the corner and down the road, Tiffany and Gil
she offered me, the guest, the swinging porch bench

I dislike the glossier paper of American Art Books
She didn't say that, but I know
Tiffany has a strabismus that must be called
severe. it took me two thirds of the time to realize i'd been looking in
her *wandered out* eye

what a relief it is to puke in the toilet
and then later be able to listen again
and think

why are they trying to convince us of these specious things?

VII.

I tried to be open about it without being disgusting
I feel nauseous, I just threw up in your bathroom
(is this a kind of lustiness?)

dreamed of two young members of the star machine
(like esther and norman from *A Star Is Born*)
who spoke to each other across the loud, crowded spaces they were often
in galas, carpets

only in animal calls
mostly alerts / reminders of presence, utterances of pleasure in possession
& alerts of pleasure in possession and utterances of presence

VIII.

on the corkboard, next to the poster for the play
she put up a flyer which contained the word *sensuous*
and her phone number sliced into strips at the bottom

Jean kept sending me short videos of earwax extraction
where this miniscule camera goes in through the cilia, down the canal
till you can see the bloodwall, a thin layer of skin thrown over a drum
(or the drum is the membrane, I can never remember)

air-sucking, the thin clear tube probes first at the sides
delicately, to pull at the thinner
skin of the bolus

> *At its best*, Jean says,
>
> > *it's like watching a beast be*
> > *wrangled from his cave*

It is disgusting
I watch it on my little phone

she said she didn't think it was disgusting at all

★

I guess I could see what she meant

★

There's something in that lightning bolt bookbag
The girl has been denied
Or deeply hates

Stop hitting it, but she is having spasms
Think about it, scratches her back dead-eyed,
bobbing

Yellow is the color of relinquishment

Yellow as a rule appears in sickness

Shone yellow through the square and narrow streets

Bobbing up like blazons in fog

On Coding Walt Whitman's Notebook

when I coded it, drew it up into the ether almost boredom mingling
with streetcars. From another round of bedside visits he'd returned.

I had practical lists. There could be no continuity to them who
discovered the yellow notebook,

If a thought not having found its end demanded a new start I'd turn
it from the back that is no beginning. Whatever page I happened to
find I'd continue, whether half-filled or sideways or far off with lists
of tasks.

Words I can't decipher, but mostly words I can. *1863*

There was a special way to code a carrot and text inserted later. Text
inserted later in pencil. And still another way to link another page,
from another time, that might explain
the impulse for revision.

When you met me I thought
The tree behind
My room was a chestnut.
It wasn't.
When I did find out the name
I used it freely
Felt
Better than the wholesome
Correspondence of one thing
To another:
Microbes, the social

Mrs. X explores the enzymes in the gut

I can feel my scapula crunching

When I think of how you must feel I get so hungry I can't move

We all sit down at the dinner
Then all of a Dryden we all get up and go bob around.

I bob around like a leg on a potato bug
Not getting touched or touching much

so I hardly had time to wipe the smile on my face
when they did the moves

I think I'll try to learn the drums

And then it's over, a relief so engrossing I put aside the notebook and
say
I will remember this night

Love won and it's horrible
I am surrounded by incomplete art.

sometimes stuff happens so fast I hardly have time to wipe the Singing
off my face, like every other child
The lifeless campfire song

★

A story of the witches:

A broad and level road led from the city
& from this another branched off to the mountain
All for the taking.

One witch jogged along mounted on an ass.
Others full of agility skipped on the ground
With as many arms as Briaereus & teeth as long as bones.

Some wore blue florescent skunktails, (butt plugs?), chokers,
purple lipstick,
& grew wet sacs of makeup out of their faces
& gnashers out of their uteri

& from each end, veiny green cocoons.

What surrenders completely to ecstasy but stays
Bouncy like a jelly?
Oh yeah, a female.

I'm young, safe, of healthy mind.
Become disoriented sometimes.
But when the film rolls I always know where to look,
Mother

Notes

Italicized words denote either thought or borrowed speech.

The argument woven through "Serial Mom" comes from Chapter 2 ("Media Hot and Cold") of Marshall McLuhan's *Understanding Media: The Extensions of Man.*

"Wings in Time"

The lines quoted from "Eric" come from a draft of Eric Linsker's poem "Dual Power," sent via email on April 9, 2020.

Text from Gustave Flaubert's *November* inspired the italicized portion ending section III: *The earth is large, I will exhaust every road, empty every horizon.*

The lines *I washed with the chemicals they gave me to wash with / I felt the feelings I was given to feel* come from Chris Nealon's *The Shore.*

"Quarantine Fascinations"

Several song and poem titles appear without quotation marks: Marie Howe's "The Seven Devils," Raffi's "Shake Your Sillies Out," Otis Redding's "Cigarettes and Coffee" (written by Jerry Butler, Eddie Thomas, and Jay Walker), Clarence Carter's "Patches" (written by General Johnson and Ron Dunbar), June Jordan's "I Must Become a Menace to My Enemies," Waxahatchee's "Lilacs" (written by Katie Crutchfield).

"That's how little babies think" modifies a line from Barack Obama's commencement speech to the class of 2020: "Doing what feels good, what's convenient, what's easy, that's how little kids think."

"Humor in Fiction"

I drag road metal is from Yeats' "The Fascination of What's Difficult."

Text from Randulf Higden's *Polychronicon* (14th C), quoted in Daniel Sherell's *Warmth*, inspired the observation on Shaw's: *Note that at the furthest reaches of the world often occur new marvels and wonders, as though Nature plays with greater freedom secretly at the edges of the world than she does openly and nearer us in the middle of it.*

Text from Diderot's *Rameau's Nephew* inspired the closing lines: *They wear everything out. Their souls run to seed and boredom takes over. In the midst of oppressive opulence it would be a kindness to relieve them of life. All they know of happiness is the part which cloys first.*

"AirBnB" takes the phrase "bringing its nervous system down to a low hum" from Sara Bissell Rubin's writing on pain, a draft of which I received via email on December 29, 2020.

"Macedonia Road" borrows *What you drink / gets into your mouth / becomes saliva* from Eric Linsker's "Mentor," a draft of which I received via email on May 17, 2020.

Lyrics by Jim Morrison from the Doors' "Break on Through" show up in "Love Street, L.A." which borrows its title from another Morrison song.

"Dear Eric" borrows *What stars there were shrunk, even as they multiplied* and *Seemed a very bad, anxious ode to redistribution* from Eric Linsker's "Two Lawyers," a draft of which I received via email on June 18, 2020.

The last two lines of "Keeping Time" are lifted, tweaked, from Hank Williams' "There's a Tear in My Beer."

The Grid of Intimacy" is named for George W. S. Trow's phrase from "Within the Context of No-Context" (1980).

"Inspiration" takes its epigraph from Agnes Martin's "The Untroubled Mind" (1972). Then it transmutes language from *The Journal of Eugéne Delacroix* ("Glory is not a vain word for me.")

"Imagination" narrates the plot of the 1988 film *Big Business*.

"On the Potential Uses of Television for the Preschool Mind" toys with language from Joan Ganz Cooney's *The Potential Uses of Television in Preschool Education*, also the source of the epigraph on page 51: https://www.joanganzcooneycenter.org/wp-content/uploads/2014/01/JGC_1966_report.pdf

Part I steals a line from Chris Nealon's *The Shore: it's like there's a scrap of glory in me I was asked to keep safe while the world goes to hell*

Part III includes a quote from an article on People.com, "Gloria Considers Gloria": https://people.com/archive/gloria-considers-gloria-vol-37-no-3/

We'll be lovers in the open comes from David Byrne's "Independence Day" (composed by Byrne, feat. Kirsty MacColl).

Acknowledgments

Mom, on behalf of all the children of *Sesame Street*, thank you for raising me.

Thank you Mom and Dad for welcoming me into your home these past months. I love you. Thank you Jean and Nick for making space for me in your family. Zuzu, this book is for you. (I hope to write you a more practical one someday, for living.) Thank you, Jo Ann, for sharing your place. Rebecca for sharing your table. Colm for finding me there.

Thank you Eric: I wrote much of this by talking to and alongside you. Thank you Dan: you drew it out of me. Thank you Adrienne, Ashley, Bridget, Colby, Katie, and Rawaan for your warmth and steadiness and incredible eyes.

Thank you Sara for showing me what's possible. Jess, for your blazing ear that made this better. Jake, you help me pull the scraps (sometimes about Helen Hunt) together. Thank you Margaret for Mendocino. How I rely on you.

Thank you Hannah, blood friend, for helping me thank media. Thank you Rob for paying attention, for your work.

Chris and Rachel, I cherish you both, and each of you, for so many reasons big and small.

My friends, I cherish you all!

Thank you to my teachers, especially Diana, Cole, Rod, Ed, Dee, and Peter.

Thank you Ben and Alan and *The Song Cave*, where I always hoped I might belong.

Gratitude to the following editors:

"Serial Mom" first appeared as part of the PEN Poetry Series. Thank you, Danniel.

"The Great San Bernardino Pitch Party" first appeared on the Poetry Foundation's website as part of their *PoetryNow* podcast series. Thank you, Michael and Katie.

Early drafts of "[A friendly looking pirate]" and "[There she goes again]" first appeared in *Pigeon Pages*. Thank you, Maddie and Hannah (and for the suggested epigraphs).

"The Grid of Intimacy" and "Inspiration" first appeared in *The Chicago Review*. Thank you, Kirsten and Steven.

OTHER TITLES FROM THE SONG CAVE:

1. *A Dark Dreambox of Another Kind* by **Alfred Starr Hamilton**

2. *My Enemies* by **Jane Gregory**

3. *Rude Woods* by **Nate Klug**

4. *Georges Braque and Others* by **Trevor Winkfield**

5. *The Living Method* by **Sara Nicholson**

6. *Splash State* by **Todd Colby**

7. *Essay Stanzas* by **Thomas Meyer**

8. *Illustrated Games of Patience* by **Ben Estes**

9. *Dark Green* by **Emily Hunt**

10. *Honest James* by **Christian Schlegel**

11. *M* by **Hannah Brooks-Motl**

12. *What the Lyric Is* by **Sara Nicholson**

13. *The Hermit* by **Lucy Ives**

14. *The Orchid Stories* by **Kenward Elmslie**

15. *Do Not Be a Gentleman When You Say Goodnight* by **Mitch Sisskind**

16. *HAIRDO* by **Rachel B. Glaser**

17. *Motor Maids across the Continent* by **Ron Padgett**

18. *Songs for Schizoid Siblings* by **Lionel Ziprin**

19. *Professionals of Hope: The Selected Writings of* **Subcomandante Marcos**

20. *Fort Not* by **Emily Skillings**

21. *Riddles, Etc.* by **Geoffrey Hilsabeck**

22. *CHARAS: The Improbable Dome Builders* by **Syeus Mottel** (Co-published with Pioneer Works)

23. *YEAH NO* by **Jane Gregory**

24. *Nioque of the Early-Spring* by **Francis Ponge**

25. *Smudgy and Lossy* by **John Myers**

26. *The Desert* by **Brandon Shimoda**

27. *Scardanelli* by **Friederike Mayröcker**

28. *The Alley of Fireflies and Other Stories* by **Raymond Roussel**

29. *CHANGES: Notes on Choreography* by **Merce Cunningham** (Co-published with the Merce Cunningham Trust)

30. *My Mother Laughs* by **Chantal Akerman**

31. *Earth* by **Hannah Brooks-Motl**

32. *Everything and Other Poems* by **Charles North**

33. *Paper Bells* by **Phan Nhiên Hạo**

34. *Photographs: Together & Alone* by **Karlheinz Weinberger**

35. *A Better Place Is Hard to Find* by **Aaron Fagan**

36. *Rough Song* by **Blanca Varela**

37. *In the Same Light: Poems For Our Century From the Migrants & Exiles of the Tang Dynasty*, translations by **Wong May**

38. *On the Mesa: An Anthology of Bolinas Writing (50th Anniversary Edition)*, edited by **Ben Estes and Joel Weishaus**

39. *Listen My Friend, This Is the Dream I Dreamed Last Night* by **Cody-Rose Clevidence**

40. *Poetries* by **Georges Schehadé**